AF477162

CAMEL AND THE SECRET OF THE SEA

CAMEL AND THE SECRET OF THE SEA

ANNIKA VIIASK
MARIA CEDERSLÄTT

www.fb-academy.com

CONTENTS

CHAPTER 1

A New Adventure Calls

In the golden desert, under the shade of an ancient palm, Camel rests alongside his friends, Aisha and Kalid, who he met at the COP28 environmental conference in Dubai.

A gentle breeze, promising adventure, carries whispers of the sea's secrets. Camel, his eyes sparkling with anticipation, breaks the silence.

"It's time for a new adventure," he announces enthusiastically. "We're off to visit my old friend, the wise sea turtle Naima. She holds deep stories about the ocean's mysteries and lurking dangers."

Aisha and Kalid's hearts race with excitement, and they quickly prepare for their next journey. Gazing towards the horizon, where the azure sea meets the sky, they dream of the secrets awaiting them.

"We'll learn so much," Aisha says, her voice full of hope, as she packs her backpack.

Kalid, ever ready for adventure, adds, "And imagine the wonders we'll see! What secrets does the ocean hide?"

As they pack, Kalid turns to Aisha, "What do you think we'll discover?"

Aisha replies with a smile, 'Something amazing, I'm sure!' Camel laughs. 'With you two by my side, every discovery will be an adventure!'

Anticipating the knowledge and discoveries that await, they mount Camel's back, their excitement growing with each step towards the coast.

They know they are embarking on a journey that will change their view of the world and deepen their understanding of nature's marvelous interplay.

And so, with hearts full of adventure and eyes reflecting the desert's golden sands, Camel leads the way to the vast, mysterious sea.

On the journey, they encounter a dried-up river blocking their path.

"How will we cross?" Aisha asks.

Kalid, inventive, suggests building a makeshift bridge. They gather palm leaves, stones, and branches, weaving them together. It isn't the prettiest bridge, but their collective effort strengthens their camaraderie and determination.

They are now one step closer to the sea.

CHAPTER 2

Meeting with the Sea Turtle

After traversing the expansive desert, where each grain of sand tells a story, Camel, Aisha, and Kalid finally reach the azure sea. They stand at the shore, where waves meet land, gazing into the endless water.

A majestic shadow appears on the horizon, moving with the grace of age and wisdom. It's Naima, the wise sea turtle, her shell marked with lines and patterns from decades of ocean voyages.

As she approaches, her eyes, filled with timeless wisdom, meet our adventurers.

"Welcome to my realm," she says, her voice echoing ancient times.

Camel, Aisha, and Kalid listen intently as Naima shares tales of vibrant but fragile underwater worlds, the treasures of coral reefs, and the creatures calling these depths home.

Naima also speaks of her travels, the currents she's navigated, and secret ocean places known only to the oldest and wisest.

For Camel, Aisha, and Kalid, meeting Naima is an eye-opener. They realize the vastness and wonder of the world beneath the waves and the importance of preserving this treasure. They are eager to absorb every word and wisdom she imparts.

When Naima speaks of ocean pollution, she turns to the children.
'What do you think, can we do something to help the sea?'
Aisha and Kalid nodded. "Yes, we can make a difference!" they say
in unison.
Camel, feeling a strong urge to act, asks, "What can we do to help,
Naima?"

Naima smiles encouragingly. "Start by telling others about meeting
me and what I've seen. We can all help by picking up plastic and other
trash, especially near water."
Kalid, brimming with energy, adds, "We can also be careful about
what we use and how we dispose of things!"

Naima nodded in approval.
"Exactly! Every little action makes
a big difference. The sea and its
creatures will thank you."

With Naima's story in their
hearts, Camel, Aisha, and Kalid
feel a strong urge to help. They
leave the beach that day with new
goals and renewed hope, ready to
make a difference in the world.

CHAPTER 3

Naima's Story

In the shadow of an ancient palm by the sea, Camel, Aisha, and Kalid sit around Naima, absorbing her stories about her years in the ocean. Naima looks at the children with eyes reflecting deep knowledge.

"The ocean is a marvelous place, full of life and color," she says. "But I've also seen things that sadden me. The water was clear, and coral reefs teemed with life. But now..."

She pauses, looking serious. "Now, nets and plastics litter the waters. Bottles, bags, and small bits mistaken for food by fish and turtles. I've seen them eat these plastics, getting sick, even dying."

Naima shares memories of a vibrant, colorful ocean, now marred by pollution.

The children, worried, ask about solutions.

Naima advises, "People often don't realize how their actions impact the ocean. But it's not too late to help."

Motivated, Aisha sketches an article, Kalid plans a beach cleanup, and Camel vows to protect the sea. Together, they commit to learning and teaching others, making a difference in preserving the ocean's beauty.

"Our journey as environmental heroes has just begun," Camel declares, as they dream of a future with clean seas, free from plastic and harm.

As night falls, Aisha and Kalid inspired by their adventure, eagerly anticipate their next mission – a quest to collect plastic bottles in the desert, unknowing of the challenges and discoveries ahead.

And so, with steps filled with anticipation and hearts full of dreams, they begin planning their next great adventure.

CHAPTER 4

A Plan for the Future

Sitting under the shady foliage of a palm at the edge of the sea, Camel, Aisha, and Kalid listen attentively to Naima, the wise sea turtle.

They are completely engrossed in her tales of the ocean's underwater world – a realm of sparkling coral reefs and playful marine creatures. But they also feel a deep concern when Naima describes how plastic entering the ocean threatens this beauty. The small pieces of plastic become a big problem in the water.

After Naima finishes her compelling story, the children are filled with a determination to make a change. They look at each other, aware that they have the power to make a difference. Aisha, sensitive and thoughtful, takes out her notebook and immediately starts sketching an article. "I want my words to make others see and understand. I want them to feel the magic of the sea and why we need to protect it," she says firmly.

Kalid, always ready to take on things practically, begins planning a beach cleaning day. "We can make it a fun and educational day! Maybe we can even turn it into a competition, see who can find the most trash," he suggests, his eyes sparkling with excitement. "We can make our beach more beautiful and safer for the animals."

Camel, whose enthusiasm is as vast as the sea, thinks about how he can spread the message. "If I am invited to your school, I can tell teachers and students about my friend Naima and our journey to the sea. I want to spread the message 'together we make a big difference'," he says, his voice filled with a passion that is unmistakable.

On their way home to the desert and their walk along the beach, they eagerly talk about their plans, each filled with a renewed sense of purpose. They discuss how Aisha's article could reach out to families and friends, how Kalid's beach cleaning could engage their local community, and how Camel's words could inspire.

With each step they take, their sense of community feels stronger, and their determination deeper. They understand that their journey has just begun, but they are ready to embrace the challenge. Together, they dream of a future where the sea is free from plastic and other dangers – a world where Naima's wonderful ocean remains as before

CHAPTER 5

Sunset Promises: The Adventure Continues

In the tender glow of the setting sun, Camel, Aisha, and Kalid stand united at the edge of the beach. Their eyes linger over the shimmering sea, waving a heartfelt farewell to Naima. A silent understanding weaves through them – it's a moment to reaffirm their vow, a solemn commitment to safeguard the mesmerizing, blue expanse before them.

Camel, with a tone imbued with resolve, proclaims, "We vow to do everything within our power to protect the sea. Each small effort contributes significantly." Aisha, her words echoing the depth of her sincerity, adds, "And we pledge to never cease learning and spreading our knowledge. Together, we can create substantial change." Kalid, nodding in firm agreement, asserts, "We promise to be proactive, to clean, and to maintain the purity of our beaches and oceans."

In a shared silence, they observe the sun's gentle descent into the ocean's embrace, a symbol of a day rich with new insights and budding hopes. They feel an intertwined strength, a united front in their mission. They recognize that every step forward, every word of advocacy, and every piece of debris they collect is pivotal in the crusade for a cleaner, healthier world.

As the day gives way to dusk, bringing a refreshing breeze against their faces, they initiate their journey home. Their minds brim with visions of the future, dreams of pristine beaches and a thriving sea. Their hearts beat with hope and unwavering determination. "Our quest as environmental champions is just beginning," Camel asserts, his gaze spanning the boundless waters. Aisha and Kalid nod in accord, and together, they embark on the path home, a path laden with challenges but also ripe with opportunities to effect real change.

"Remember," Camel intones as he bids the children goodbye at their doorstep, "next time we convene, it's your turn to choose our next environmental escapade!"

As Aisha and Kalid stroll homeward, their conversation bubbles with excitement over their experiences. They reminisce about the wise sea turtle, her tales of the sea and its inhabitants, the plight of plastic pollution, and her enduring hope ignited by the youth's desire to better the environment.

But as nightfall cloaks the sky and the first stars begin to twinkle, Aisha suddenly proposes, "What if we embark on a Bottle Return Adventure for Camel?" Kalid, reflecting on the idea, responds, "It's going to be an unforgettable journey!"

Oblivious to the challenges and revelations that await them, Aisha, and Kalid brim with anticipation.

And so, with steps buoyed by expectation and hearts laden with dreams, they commence planning their next grand adventure – a quest to collect PET bottles in the desert, which they will then take to the bottle return station. What adventures lie ahead among the desert's fauna and warm dunes, and how will Camel react to their mission? This is a tale yet to unfold... another day.

CHAPTER 6

A Guide for young ocean protectors - Understanding plastic in the ocean

Imagine a plastic bottle that takes more than 400 years to completely break down! During this time, it can be very harmful to many sea animals and plants. Sometimes, animals mistake plastic for food, which can make them very sick, and sadly, it can even cause them to die. As plastic breaks down, it turns into tiny pieces called microplastics. These little pieces are hard to see but can pollute the water greatly. In some parts of the sea, there's so much plastic and trash gathered together in one area, like the Great Pacific Garbage Patch, which is larger than many countries!

Reducing plastic in the sea might seem like a big task, but there are many things we can do:

Use reusable products:

Instead of using plastic items that are thrown away after one use (like plastic bags and bottles), we can use things that can be used many times. Cloth bags, metal or glass bottles, and reusable lunch boxes are great choices.

Join cleanup activities:

We can help clean beaches, rivers, and other places near water. Picking up plastic and other trash keeps it from getting into the sea.

Recycle wisely:

Learn about which plastic items can be recycled and how to recycle them properly. Recycling helps reduce the amount of plastic that ends up harming nature.

Choose less plastic when shopping:

Try to buy things that aren't wrapped in plastic. For example, choose fruits and vegetables without plastic packaging or look for products in paper packaging.

Share your knowledge:

Talk to your family, friends, and others about the problem of plastic in the sea and how they can help. The more people understand, the more they can do to help.

Why Is This Important?

The oceans and the seas are like a big house for millions of animals and plants, and their health is very important for the whole planet. When beaches and seas are clean, we can enjoy nature without worrying about trash and pollution. By keeping the sea free from plastic, we are helping sea creatures, ourselves, and even people who will live on our planet in the future. Taking care of the sea means taking care of our Earth and everyone who shares it with us.

Remember, every small action you take can make a big difference in keeping our oceans healthy and beautiful!

About the Authors

Annika Viiask

Annika is a certified teacher and has been in the profession for nearly 30 years. She has worked with children of various ages, including those with special needs. Annika has a strong commitment to environmental issues and has been head of charge of the school's environmental initiatives for 20 years.

Maria Cederslätt

Maria has a background in education and childcare for more than 30 years, while Mia is a skilled illustrator with a strong passion for environmental issues. She breathes life into the stories through her vibrant and impactful artwork, creating all the illustrations for the tales.

This is the second book in the children's book series where we meet Camel, Alisha, and Kalid. The first book in the series, 'The Hunt for the Rainbow Treasure,' was first published in January 2024.

FB Academy

Our mission serves as an anchor of optimism and actionable change. We're not just committed to **sustainable development** as an abstract concept, but as a **concrete roadmap** to a better future.

However, **education, knowledge and learning are the basis for all development**. Our methodology is based on science and proven methods combined with the latest digital technology.

Visit http://www.fb-academy.com for more information and inspiration about our learning platform.